Japanese Fairy Tales

EDITED BY PHILIP SMITH

Illustrated by Kakuzo Fujiyama

DOVER PUBLICATIONS, INC.
New York

DOVER CHILDREN'S THRIFT CLASSICS
EDITOR: PHILIP SMITH

Copyright © 1992 by Dover Publications, Inc.
All rights reserved under Pan American and International Copyright Conventions.

Published in Canada by General Publishing Company, Ltd., 30 Lesmill Road, Don Mills, Toronto, Ontario.
Published in the United Kingdom by Constable and Company, Ltd., 3 The Lanchesters, 162–164 Fulham Palace Road, London W6 9ER.

Japanese Fairy Tales, first published by Dover Publications, Inc., in 1992, is a new selection of five tales from *The Japanese Fairy Book*, compiled by Yei Theodora Ozaki, originally published by Archibald Constable & Co. Ltd., Westminster, England, in 1903. The illustrations are taken from the original edition. A new Note has been specially written for the Dover edition.

Manufactured in the United States of America
Dover Publications, Inc., 31 East 2nd Street, Mineola, N.Y. 11501

Library of Congress Cataloging-in-Publication Data

Japanese fairy book. Selections.
    Japanese fairy tales / edited by Philip Smith ; illustrated by Kakuzo Fujiyama.
        p.   cm. — (Dover children's thrift classics)
    "Selection of five tales from the Japanese fairy book, compiled by Yei Theodora Ozaki, originally published by Archibald Constable & Co. Ltd., Westminster, England, in 1903"—T.p. verso.
    Summary: Includes five fairy tales derived from centuries-old popular stories told in Japan, stressing such attitudes as respect, obedience, courage, and integrity.
    ISBN 0-486-27300-8 (pbk.)
    1. Fairy tales—Japan. [1. Fairy tales. 2. Folklore—Japan.] I. Smith, Philip, 1967–   . II. Fujiyama, Kakuzō, ill. III. Ozaki, Yei Theodora. IV. Title. V. Series.
PZ8.J2625 1992
398.21'0952—dc20
[E]   92–17648
                                                           CIP
                                                            AC

Note

Although today a highly industrialized nation playing an important role in the global economy, Japan was not widely subjected to Western technology and influences until the mid-1800s, when a centuries-old policy of cultural isolationism came to an end. Prior to that time Japanese culture flourished in distinctive traditions of great strength and delicacy that had their own unique structures, customs and aesthetics—traditions that continue to shape much of Japanese life.

The fairy tales in this book, which were collected a few decades following Japan's opening to the West, are derived from popular stories told in Japan for centuries. Some refer to leaders and events in Japanese history dating back nearly a thousand years. These stories, like Western fairy tales, frequently stress moral standards important to their society, especially respect and obedience to parents and authority figures, courage and keeping one's word.

This collection is complemented by traditional Japanese ink-brush illustrations, which, like the stories, reflect the singular beauty of old Japan.

Contents

List of Illustrations

Momotaro, or the Story
of the Son of a Peach

L ONG, LONG AGO there lived an old man
and an old woman; they were peasants,
and had to work hard to earn their daily rice.
The old man used to go and cut grass for the
farmers around, and while he was gone the
old woman, his wife, did the work of the
house and worked in their own little rice field.

One day the old man went to the hills as
usual to cut grass and the old woman took
some clothes to the river to wash.

It was nearly summer, and the country was
very beautiful to see in its fresh greenness as
the two old people went on their way to work.
The grass on the banks of the river looked
like emerald velvet, and the pussy willows
along the edge of the water were shaking out
their soft tassels.

The breezes blew and ruffled the smooth
surface of the water into wavelets, and passing on touched the cheeks of the old couple

who, for some reason they could not explain, felt very happy that morning.

The old woman at last found a nice spot by the river bank and put her basket down. Then she set to work to wash the clothes; she took them one by one out of the basket and washed them in the river and rubbed them on the stones. The water was as clear as crystal, and she could see the tiny fish swimming to and fro, and the pebbles at the bottom.

As she was busy washing her clothes a great peach came bumping down the stream. The old woman looked up from her work and saw this large peach. She was sixty years of

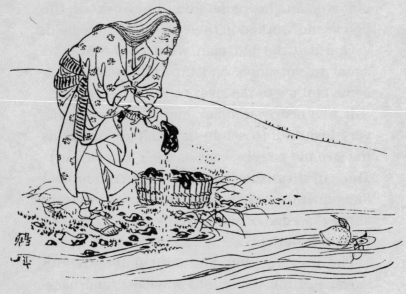

She set to work to wash the clothes.

age, yet in all her life she had never seen such a big peach as this.

"How delicious that peach must be!" she said to herself. "I must certainly get it and take it home to my old man."

She stretched out her arm to try and get it, but it was quite out of her reach. She looked about for a stick, but there was not one to be seen, and if she went to look for one she would lose the peach.

Stopping a moment to think what she would do, she remembered an old charm-verse. Now she began to clap her hands to keep time to the rolling of the peach down stream, and while she clapped she sang this song:

> "Distant water is bitter,
> The near water is sweet;
> Pass by the distant water
> And come into the sweet."

Strange to say, as soon as she began to repeat this little song the peach began to come nearer and nearer the bank where the old woman was standing, till at last it stopped just in front of her so that she was able to take it up in her hands. The old woman was delighted. She could not go on with her work, so happy and excited was she, so she put all the clothes back in her bamboo basket, and with the basket on her back and the peach in her hand she hurried homewards.

It seemed a very long time to her to wait till her husband returned. The old man at last came back as the sun was setting, with a big bundle of grass on his back—so big that he was almost hidden and she could hardly see him. He seemed very tired and used the scythe for a walking stick, leaning on it as he walked along.

As soon as the old woman saw him she called out:

"O Jii San! (old man) I have been waiting for you to come home for such a long time to-day!"

"What is the matter? Why are you so impatient?" asked the old man, wondering at her unusual eagerness. "Has anything happened while I have been away?"

"Oh, no!" answered the old woman, "nothing has happened, only I have found a nice present for you!"

"That is good," said the old man. He then washed his feet in a basin of water and stepped up to the verandah.

The old woman now ran into the little room and brought out from the cupboard the big peach. It felt even heavier than before. She held it up to him, saying:

"Just look at this! Did you ever see such a large peach in all your life?"

When the old man looked at the peach he was greatly astonished and said:

"This is indeed the largest peach I have ever seen! Wherever did you buy it?"

"I did not buy it," answered the old woman. "I found it in the river where I was washing." And she told him the whole story.

"I am very glad that you have found it. Let us eat it now, for I am hungry," said the O Jii San.

He brought out the kitchen knife, and, placing the peach on a board, was about to cut it when, wonderful to tell, the peach split in two of itself and a clear voice said:

"Wait a bit, old man!" and out stepped a beautiful little child.

The old man and his wife were both so astonished at what they saw that they fell to the ground. The child spoke again:

"Don't be afraid. I am no demon or fairy. I will tell you the truth. Heaven has had compassion on you. Every day and every night you have lamented that you had no child. Your cry has been heard and I am sent to be the son of your old age!"

On hearing this the old man and his wife were very happy. They had cried night and day for sorrow at having no child to help

The peach split in two of itself.

them in their lonely old age, and now that their prayer was answered they were so lost with joy that they did not know where to put their hands or their feet. First the old man took the child up in his arms, and then the old woman did the same; and they named him Momotaro, or Son of a Peach, because he had come out of a peach.

The years passed quickly by and the child grew to be fifteen years of age. He was taller and far stronger then any other boys of his own age, he had a handsome face and a heart full of courage, and he was very wise for his years. The old couple's pleasure was very great when they looked at him, for he was just what they thought a hero ought to be like.

One day Momotaro came to his foster-father and said solemnly:

"Father, by a strange chance we have become father and son. Your goodness to me has been higher than the mountain grasses which it was your daily work to cut, and deeper than the river where my mother washes the clothes. I do not know how to thank you enough."

"Why," answered the old man, "it is a matter of course that a father should bring up his son. When you are older it will be your turn to take care of us, so after all there will be no

profit or loss between us—all will be equal.
Indeed, I am rather surprised that you should
thank me in this way!" and the old man
looked bothered.

"I hope you will be patient with me," said
Momotaro; "but before I begin to pay back
your goodness to me I have a request to make
which I hope you will grant me above everything else."

"I will let you do whatever you wish, for
you are quite different to all other boys!"

"Then let me go away at once!"

"What do you say? Do you wish to leave
your old father and mother and go away from
your old home?"

"I will surely come back again, if you let me
go now!"

"Where are you going?"

"You must think it strange that I want to go
away," said Momotaro, "because I have not
yet told you my reason. Far away from here to
the north-east of Japan there is an island in
the sea. This island is the stronghold of a
band of devils. I have often heard how they
invade this land, kill and rob the people, and
carry off all they can find. They are not only
very wicked but they are disloyal to our
Emperor and disobey his laws. They are also
cannibals, for they kill and eat some of the
poor people who are so unfortunate as to fall

into their hands. These devils are very hateful beings. I must go and conquer them and bring back all the plunder of which they have robbed this land. It is for this reason that I want to go away for a short time!"

The old man was much surprised at hearing all this from a mere boy of fifteen. He thought it best to let the boy go. He was strong and fearless, and besides all this, the old man knew he was no common child, for he had been sent to them as a gift from Heaven, and he felt quite sure that the devils would be powerless to harm him.

"All you say is very interesting, Momotaro," said the old man. "I will not hinder you in your determination. You may go if you wish. Go to the island as soon as ever you like and destroy the demons and bring peace to the land."

"Thank you, for all your kindness," said Momotaro, who began to get ready to go that very day. He was full of courage and did not know what fear was.

The old man and woman at once set to work to pound rice in the kitchen mortar to make cakes for Momotaro to take with him on his journey.

At last the cakes were made and Momotaro ready to start on his long journey.

Parting is always sad. So it was now. The

eyes of the two old people were filled with tears and their voices trembled as they said:

"Go with all care and speed. We expect you back victorious!"

Momotaro was very sorry to leave his old parents, (though he knew he was coming back as soon as he could) for he thought of how lonely they would be while he was away. But he said "Good-bye!" quite bravely.

"I am going now. Take good care of yourselves while I am away. Good-bye!" And he stepped quickly out of the house. In silence the eyes of Momotaro and his parents met in farewell.

Momotaro now hurried on his way till it was midday. He began to feel hungry, so he opened his bag and took out one of the rice-cakes and sat down under a tree by the side of the road to eat it. While he was thus having his lunch a dog almost as large as a colt came running out from the high grass. He made straight for Momotaro, and showing his teeth, said in a fierce way:

"You are a rude man to pass my field without asking permission first. If you leave me all the cakes you have in your bag you may go; otherwise I will bite you till I kill you!"

Momotaro only laughed scornfully:

"What is that you are saying? Do you know

who I am? I am Momotaro, and I am on my way to subdue the devils in their island stronghold in the north-east of Japan. If you try to stop me on my way there I will cut you in two from the head downwards!"

The dog's manner at once changed. His tail dropped between his legs, and coming near he bowed so low that his forehead touched the ground.

"What do I hear? The name of Momotaro? Are you indeed Momotaro? I have often heard of your great strength. Not knowing who you were I have behaved in a very stupid way. Will you please pardon my rudeness? Are you indeed on your way to invade the Island of Devils? If you will take such a rude fellow with you as one of your followers, I shall be very grateful to you."

"I think I can take you with me if you wish to go," said Momotaro.

"Thank you!" said the dog. "By the way, I am very very hungry. Will you give me one of the cakes you are carrying?"

"This is the best kind of cake there is in Japan," said Momotaro. "I cannot spare you a whole one; I will give you half of one."

"Thank you very much," said the dog, taking the piece thrown to him.

Then Momotaro got up and the dog followed. For a long time they walked over the hills and through the valleys. As they were going along an animal came down from a tree a little ahead of them. The creature soon came up to Momotaro and said:

"Good morning, Momotaro! You are welcome in this part of the country. Will you allow me to go with you?"

The dog answered jealously:

"Momotaro already has a dog to accompany him. Of what use is a monkey like you in battle? We are on our way to fight the devils! Get away!"

The dog and the monkey began to quarrel and bite, for these two animals always hate each other.

"Now, don't quarrel!" said Momotaro, putting himself between them. "Wait a moment, dog!"

"It is not at all dignified for you to have such a creature as that following you!" said the dog.

"What do you know about it?" asked Momotaro; and pushing aside the dog, he spoke to the monkey:

"Who are you?"

"I am a monkey living in these hills," replied the monkey. "I heard of your expedition to the Island of Devils, and I have come to go with

you. Nothing will please me more than to follow you!"

"Do you really wish to go to the Island of
Devils and fight with me?"

"Yes, sir," replied the monkey.

"I admire your courage," said Momotaro.
"Here is a piece of one of my fine rice-cakes.
Come along!"

So the monkey joined Momotaro. The dog
and the monkey did not get on well together.
They were always snapping at each other as
they went along, and always wanting to have
a fight. This made Momotaro very cross, and
at last he sent the dog on ahead with a flag
and put the monkey behind with a sword, and
he placed himself between them with a war-
fan, which is made of iron.

By-and-bye they came to a large field. Here
a bird flew down and alighted on the ground
just in front of the little party. It was the most
beautiful bird Momotaro had ever seen. On its
body were five different robes of feathers and
its head was covered with a scarlet cap.

The dog at once ran at the bird and tried to
seize and kill it. But the bird struck out its
spurs and flew at the dog's tail, and the fight
went hard with both.

Momotaro, as he looked on, could not help
admiring the bird; it showed so much spirit in

the fight. It would certainly make a good fighter.

Momotaro went up to the two combatants, and holding the dog back, said to the bird:

"You rascal! you are hindering my journey. Surrender at once, and I will take you with me. If you don't I will set this dog to bite your head off!"

Then the bird surrendered at once, and begged to be taken into Momotaro's company.

"I do not know what excuse to offer for quarrelling with the dog, your servant, but I did not see you. I am a miserable bird called a pheasant. It is very generous of you to pardon my rudeness and to take me with you. Please allow me to follow you behind the dog and the monkey!"

"I congratulate you on surrendering so soon," said Momotaro, smiling. "Come and join us in our raid on the devils."

"Are you going to take this bird with you also?" asked the dog, interrupting.

"Why do you ask such an unnecessary question? Didn't you hear what I said? I take the bird with me because I wish to!"

"Humph!" said the dog.

Then Momotaro stood and gave this order:

"Now all of you must listen to me. The first thing necessary in an army is harmony. It is a wise saying which says that 'Advantage on earth is better than advantage in Heaven!' Union amongst ourselves is better than any earthly gain. When we are not at peace amongst ourselves it is no easy thing to subdue an enemy. From now, you three, the dog, the monkey and the pheasant, must be friends with one mind. The one who first begins a quarrel will be discharged on the spot!"

All the three promised not to quarrel. The pheasant was now made a member of Momotaro's suite, and received half a cake.

Momotaro's influence was so great that the three became good friends, and hurried onwards with him as their leader.

Hurrying on day after day they at last came out upon the shore of the North-Eastern Sea. There was nothing to be seen as far as the horizon—not a sign of any island. All that broke the stillness was the rolling of the waves upon the shore.

Now, the dog and the monkey and the pheasant had come very bravely all the way through the long valleys and over the hills, but they had never seen the sea before, and for the first time since they set out they were bewildered and gazed at each other in silence. How were they to cross the water and get to the Island of Devils?

Momotaro soon saw that they were daunted by the sight of the sea, and to try them he spoke loudly and roughly:

"Why do you hesitate? Are you afraid of the sea? Oh! what cowards you are! It is impossible to take such weak creatures as you with me to fight the demons. It will be far better for me to go alone. I discharge you all at once!"

The three animals were taken aback at this sharp reproof, and clung to Momotaro's sleeve, begging him not to send them away.

"Please, Momotaro!" said the dog.

"We have come thus far!" said the monkey.

"It is inhuman to leave us here!" said the pheasant.

"We are not at all afraid of the sea," said the monkey again.

"Please do take us with you," said the pheasant.

"Do, please," said the dog.

They had now gained a little courage, so Momotaro said:

"Well, then, I will take you with me, but be careful!"

Momotaro now got a small ship, and they all got on board. The wind and weather were fair, and the ship went like an arrow over the sea. It was the first time they had ever been on the water, and so at first the dog, the monkey and the pheasant were frightened at the waves and the rolling of the vessel, but by degrees they grew accustomed to the water and were quite happy again. Every day they paced the deck of their little ship, eagerly looking out for the demons' island.

When they grew tired of this, they told each other stories of all their exploits of which they were proud, and then played games together; and Momotaro found much to amuse him in listening to the three animals and watching their antics, and in this way he forgot that the way was long and that he was tired of the voyage and of doing nothing. He longed to be at work killing the monsters who had done so much harm in his country.

As the wind blew in their favour and they met no storms the ship made a quick voyage, and one day when the sun was shining brightly a sight of land rewarded the four watchers at the bow.

Momotaro knew at once that what they saw was the devils' stronghold. On the top of the precipitous shore, looking out to sea, was a large castle. Now that his enterprise was close at hand, he was deep in thought with his head leaning on his hands, wondering how he should begin the attack. His three followers watched him, waiting for orders. At last he called to the pheasant:

"It is a great advantage for us to have you with us," said Momotaro to the bird, "for you have good wings. Fly at once to the castle and engage the demons to fight. We will follow you."

The pheasant at once obeyed. He flew off from the ship beating the air gladly with his wings. The bird soon reached the island and took up his position on the roof in the middle of the castle, calling out loudly:

"All you devils listen to me! The great Japanese general Momotaro has come to fight you and to take your stronghold from you. If you wish to save your lives surrender at once, and in token of your submission you must break off the horns that grow on your forehead. If you do not surrender at once, but make up your mind to fight, we, the pheasant, the dog and the monkey, will kill you all by biting and tearing you to death!"

The horned demons looking up and only seeing a pheasant, laughed and said:

"A wild pheasant, indeed! It is ridiculous to hear such words from a mean thing like you. Wait till you get a blow from one of our iron bars!"

Very angry, indeed, were the devils. They

shook their horns and their shocks of red hair fiercely, and rushed to put on tiger skin trousers to make themselves look more terrible. They then brought out great iron bars and ran to where the pheasant perched over their heads, and tried to knock him down. The pheasant flew to one side to escape the blow, and then attacked the head of first one and then another demon. He flew round and round them, beating the air with his wings so fiercely and ceaselessly, that the devils began to wonder whether they had to fight one or many more birds.

In the meantime, Momotaro had brought his ship to land. As they had approached, he saw that the shore was like a precipice, and that the large castle was surrounded by high walls and large iron gates and was strongly fortified.

Momotaro landed, and with the hope of finding some way of entrance, walked up the path towards the top, followed by the monkey and the dog. They soon came upon two beautiful damsels washing clothes in a stream. Momotaro saw that the clothes were blood-stained, and that as the two maidens washed, the tears were falling fast down their cheeks. He stopped and spoke to them:

"Who are you, and why do you weep?"

"We are captives of the Demon King. We were carried away from our homes to this island, and though we are the daughters of Daimios (Lords), we are obliged to be his servants, and one day he will kill us"—and the maidens held up the blood-stained clothes— "and eat us, and there is no one to help us!"

And their tears burst out afresh at this horrible thought.

"I will rescue you," said Momotaro. "Do not weep any more, only show me how I may get into the castle."

Then the two ladies led the way and showed Momotaro a little back door in the lowest part of the castle wall—so small that Momotaro could hardly crawl in.

The pheasant, who was all this time fighting hard, saw Momotaro and his little band rush in at the back.

Momotaro's onslaught was so furious that the devils could not stand against him. At first their foe had been a single bird, the pheasant, but now that Momotaro and the dog and the monkey had arrived they were bewildered, for the four enemies fought like a hundred, so strong were they. Some of the devils fell off the parapet of the castle and were dashed to pieces on the rocks beneath; others fell into the sea and were drowned; many were beaten to death by the three animals.

The chief of the devils at last was the only one left. He made up his mind to surrender, for he knew that his enemy was stronger than mortal man.

He came up humbly to Momotaro and threw down his iron bar, and kneeling down at the victor's feet he broke off the horns on his head in token of submission, for they were the sign of his strength and power.

"I am afraid of you," he said meekly. "I cannot stand against you. I will give you all the treasure hidden in this castle if you will spare my life!"

Momotaro laughed.

"It is not like you, big devil, to beg for mercy, is it? I cannot spare your wicked life, however much you beg, for you have killed and tortured many people and robbed our country for many years."

Then Momotaro tied the devil chief up and gave him into the monkey's charge. Having done this, he went into all the rooms of the castle and set the prisoners free and gathered together all the treasure he found.

The dog and the pheasant carried home the plunder, and thus Momotaro returned triumphantly to his home, taking with him the devil chief as a captive.

The two poor damsels, daughters of Daimios, and others whom the wicked demon

Momotaro returned triumphantly to his home.

had carried off to be his slaves, were taken safely to their own homes and delivered to their parents.

The whole country made a hero of Momotaro on his triumphant return, and rejoiced that the country was now freed from the robber devils who had been a terror of the land for a long time.

The old couple's joy was greater than ever, and the treasure Momotaro had brought home with him enabled them to live in peace and plenty to the end of their days.

The Tongue-cut
Sparrow

LONG, LONG AGO in Japan there lived an old man and his wife. The old man was a good, kind-hearted, hard-working old fellow, but his wife was a regular cross-patch, who spoilt the happiness of her home by her scolding tongue. She was always grumbling about something from morning to night. The old man had for a long time ceased to take any notice of her crossness. He was out most of the day at work in the fields, and as he had no child, for his amusement when he came home, he kept a tame sparrow. He loved the little bird just as much as if she had been his child.

When he came back at night after his hard day's work in the open air it was his only pleasure to pet the sparrow, to talk to her and to teach her little tricks, which she learned very quickly. The old man would open her cage and let her fly about the room, and they would play together. Then when supper-time came, he always saved some tit-bits from his meal with which to feed his little bird.

Now one day the old man went out to chop wood in the forest, and the old woman stopped at home to wash clothes. The day before, she had made some starch, and now when she came to look for it, it was all gone; the bowl which she had filled full yesterday was quite empty.

While she was wondering who could have used or stolen the starch, down flew the pet sparrow, and bowing her little feathered head—a trick which she had been taught by her master—the pretty bird chirped and said:

"It is I who have taken the starch. I thought it was some food put out for me in that basin, and I ate it all. If I have made a mistake I beg you to forgive me! tweet, tweet, tweet!"

You see from this that the sparrow was a truthful bird, and the old woman ought to have been willing to forgive her at once when she asked her pardon so nicely. But not so.

The old woman had never loved the sparrow, and had often quarrelled with her husband for keeping what she called a dirty bird about the house, saying that it only made extra work for her. Now she was only too delighted to have some cause of complaint against the pet. She scolded and even cursed the poor little bird for her bad behaviour, and not content with using these harsh, unfeeling words, in a fit of rage she seized the sparrow—who all this time had spread out her wings and bowed her head before the old woman, to show how sorry she was—and fetched the scissors and cut off the poor little bird's tongue.

"I suppose you took my starch with that tongue! Now you may see what it is like to go without it!" And with these dreadful words she drove the bird away, not caring in the least what might happen to it and without the smallest pity for its suffering, so unkind was she!

The old woman, after she had driven the sparrow away, made some more rice-paste, grumbling all the time at the trouble, and after starching all her clothes, spread the things on boards to dry in the sun, instead of ironing them as they do in England.

In the evening the old man came home. As usual, on the way back he looked forward to the time when he should reach his gate and see his pet come flying and chirping to meet him, ruffling out her feathers to show her joy, and at last coming to rest on his shoulder. But to-night the old man was very disappointed, for not even the shadow of his dear sparrow was to be seen.

He quickened his steps, hastily drew off his

And with these dreadful words she drove the bird away.

straw sandals, and stepped on to the verandah. Still no sparrow was to be seen. He now
felt sure that his wife, in one of her cross tem-
pers, had shut the sparrow up in its cage. So
he called her and said anxiously:

"Where is Suzume San (Miss Sparrow) to-
day?"

The old woman pretended not to know at
first, and answered:

"Your sparrow? I am sure I don't know.
Now I come to think of it, I haven't seen her
all the afternoon. I shouldn't wonder if the
ungrateful bird had flown away and left you
after all your petting!"

But at last, when the old man gave her no
peace, but asked her again and again, insisting
that she must know what had happened to his
pet, she confessed all. She told him crossly
how the sparrow had eaten the rice-paste she
had specially made for starching her clothes,
and how when the sparrow had confessed to
what she had done, in great anger she had
taken her scissors and cut out her tongue, and
how finally she had driven the bird away and
forbidden her to return to the house again.

Then the old woman showed her husband
the sparrow's tongue, saying:

"Here is the tongue I cut off! Horrid little
bird, why did it eat all my starch?"

"How could you be so cruel? Oh! how could you be so cruel?" was all that the old man could answer. He was too kind-hearted to punish his shrew of a wife, but he was terribly distressed at what had happened to his poor little sparrow.

"What a dreadful misfortune for my poor Suzume San to lose her tongue!" he said to himself. "She won't be able to chirp any more, and surely the pain of the cutting of it out in that rough way must have made her ill! Is there nothing to be done?"

The old man shed many tears after his cross wife had gone to sleep. While he wiped away the tears with the sleeve of his cotton robe, a bright thought comforted him: he would go and look for the sparrow on the morrow. Having decided this he was able to go to sleep at last.

The next morning he rose early, as soon as ever the day broke, and snatching a hasty breakfast, started out over the hills and through the woods, stopping at every clump of bamboos to cry:

"Where, oh where does my tongue-cut sparrow stay? Where, oh where, does my tongue-cut sparrow stay?"

He never stopped to rest for his noonday meal, and it was far on in the afternoon when he found himself near a large bamboo wood.

Bamboo groves are the favourite haunts of sparrows, and there sure enough at the edge of the wood he saw his own dear sparrow waiting to welcome him. He could hardly believe his eyes for joy, and ran forward quickly to greet her. She bowed her little head and went through a number of the tricks her master had taught her, to show her pleasure at seeing her old friend again, and, wonderful to relate, she could talk as of old. The old man told her how sorry he was for all that had happened, and inquired after her tongue, wondering how she could speak so well without it. Then the sparrow opened her beak and showed him that a new tongue had grown in place of the old one, and begged him not to think any more about the past, for she was quite well now. Then the old man knew that his sparrow was a fairy, and no common bird. It would be difficult to exaggerate the old man's rejoicing now. He forgot all his troubles, he forgot even how tired he was, for he had found his lost sparrow, and instead of being ill and without a tongue as he had feared and expected to find her, she was well and happy and with a new tongue, and without a sign of the ill-treatment she had received from his wife. And above all she was a fairy.

The sparrow asked him to follow her, and

flying before him she led him to a beautiful house in the heart of the bamboo grove. The old man was utterly astonished when he entered the house to find what a beautiful place it was. It was built of the whitest wood, the soft cream-coloured mats which took the place of carpets were the finest he had ever seen, and the cushions that the sparrow brought out for him to sit on were made of the finest silk and crape. Beautiful vases and lacquer boxes adorned the *tokonoma*[1] of every room.

The sparrow led the old man to the place of honour, and then, taking her place at a humble distance, she thanked him with many polite bows for all the kindness he had shown her for many long years.

Then the Lady Sparrow, as we will now call her, introduced all her family to the old man. This done, her daughters, robed in dainty crape gowns, brought in on beautiful old-fashioned trays a feast of all kinds of delicious foods, till the old man began to think he must be dreaming. In the middle of the dinner some of the sparrow's daughters performed a wonderful dance, called the *"Suzume-odori"* or the "Sparrow's dance," to amuse the guest.

[1] An alcove where precious objects are displayed.

The Lady Sparrow introduced all her family.

Never had the old man enjoyed himself so much. The hours flew by too quickly in this lovely spot, with all these fairy sparrows to wait upon him and to feast him and to dance before him.

But the night came on and the darkness reminded him that he had a long way to go and must think about taking his leave and return home. He thanked his kind hostess for her splendid entertainment, and begged her for his sake to forget all she had suffered at the hands of his cross old wife. He told the Lady Sparrow that it was a great comfort and happiness to him to find her in such a beauti-

ful home and to know that she wanted for
nothing. It was his anxiety to know how she
fared and what had really happened to her
that had led him to seek her. Now he knew
that all was well he could return home with a
light heart. If ever she wanted him for anything she had only to send for him and he
would come at once.

The Lady Sparrow begged him to stay and
rest several days and enjoy the change, but
the old man said that he must return to his old
wife—who would probably be cross at his not
coming home at the usual time—and to his
work, and therefore, much as he wished to do
so, he could not accept her kind invitation.
But now that he knew where the Lady Sparrow lived he would come to see her whenever
he had the time.

When the Lady Sparrow saw that she could
not persuade the old man to stay longer, she
gave an order to some of her servants, and
they at once brought in two boxes, one large
and the other small. These were placed before
the old man, and the Lady Sparrow asked him
to choose whichever he liked for a present,
which she wished to give him.

The old man could not refuse this kind pro-
posal, and he chose the smaller box, saying:

"I am now too old and feeble to carry the

big and heavy box. As you are so kind as to say that I may take whichever I like, I will choose the small one, which will be easier for me to carry."

Then the sparrows all helped him put it on his back and went to the gate to see him off, bidding him good-bye with many bows and entreating him to come again whenever he had the time. Thus the old man and his pet sparrow separated quite happily, the sparrow showing not the least ill-will for all the unkindness she had suffered at the hands of the old wife. Indeed, she only felt sorrow for the old man who had to put up with it all his life.

When the old man reached home he found his wife even crosser than usual, for it was late on in the night and she had been waiting up for him for a long time.

"Where have you been all this time?" she asked in a big voice. "Why do you come back so late?"

The old man tried to pacify her by showing her the box of presents he had brought back with him, and then he told her of all that had happened to him, and how wonderfully he had been entertained at the sparrow's house.

"Now let us see what is in the box," said the old man, not giving her time to grumble again.

"You must help me open it." And they both sat down before the box and opened it.

To their utter astonishment they found the box filled to the brim with gold and silver coins and many other precious things. The mats of their little cottage fairly glittered as they took out the things one by one and put them down and handled them over and over again. The old man was overjoyed at the sight of the riches that were now his. Beyond his brightest expectations was the sparrow's gift, which would enable him to give up work and live in ease and comfort the rest of his days.

He said: "Thanks to my good little sparrow! Thanks to my good little sparrow!" many times.

But the old woman, after the first moments of surprise and satisfaction at the sight of the gold and silver were over, could not suppress the greed of her wicked nature. She now began to reproach the old man for not having brought home the big box of presents, for in the innocence of his heart he had told her how he had refused the large box of presents which the sparrows had offered him, preferring the smaller one because it was light and easy to carry home.

"You silly old man," said she, "why did you not bring the large box? Just think what we have lost. We might have had twice as much silver and gold as this. You are certainly an old fool!" she screamed, and then went to bed as angry as she could be.

The old man now wished that he had said nothing about the big box, but it was too late; the greedy old woman, not contented with the good luck which had so unexpectedly befallen them and which she so little deserved, made up her mind, if possible, to get more.

Early the next morning she got up and made the old man describe the way to the sparrow's house. When he saw what was in her mind he tried to keep her from going, but it was useless. She would not listen to one word he said. It is strange that the old woman did not feel ashamed of going to see the sparrow after the cruel way she had treated her in cutting off her tongue in a fit of rage. But her greed to get the big box made her forget everything else. It did not even enter her thoughts that the sparrows might be angry with her—as, indeed, they were—and might punish her for what she had done.

Ever since the Lady Sparrow had returned home in the sad plight in which they had first found her, weeping and bleeding from the mouth, her whole family and relations had done little else but speak of the cruelty of the old woman. "How could she," they asked each other, "inflict such a heavy punishment for such a trifling offence as that of eating some rice-paste by mistake?" They all loved the old man who was so kind and good and patient under all his troubles, but the old woman they hated, and they determined, if ever they had the chance, to punish her as she deserved. They had not long to wait.

After walking for some hours the old woman had at last found the bamboo grove which she had made her husband carefully describe, and now she stood before it crying out:

"Where is the tongue-cut sparrow's house? Where is the tongue-cut sparrow's house?"

At last she saw the eaves of the house peeping out from amongst the bamboo foliage. She hastened to the door and knocked loudly.

When the servants told the Lady Sparrow that her old mistress was at the door asking to see her, she was somewhat surprised at the unexpected visit, after all that had taken place, and she wondered not a little at the boldness of the old woman in venturing to come to the house. The Lady Sparrow, however, was a polite bird, and so she went out to greet the old woman, remembering that she had once been her mistress.

The old woman intended, however, to waste no time in words, she went right to the point, without the least shame, and said:

"You need not trouble to entertain me as you did my old man. I have come myself to get the box which he so stupidly left behind. I shall soon take my leave if you will give me the big box—that is all I want!"

The Lady Sparrow at once consented, and told her servants to bring out the big box. The old woman eagerly seized it and hoisted it on her back, and without even stopping to thank the Lady Sparrow began to hurry homewards.

The box was so heavy that she could not walk fast, much less run, as she would have liked to do, so anxious was she to get home and see what was inside the box, but she had often to sit down and rest herself by the way.

While she was staggering along under the heavy load, her desire to open the box became too great to be resisted. She could wait no longer, for she supposed this box to be full of gold and silver and precious jewels like the small one her husband had received.

At last this greedy and selfish old woman put down the box by the wayside and opened it carefully, expecting to gloat her eyes on a mine of wealth. What she saw, however, so terrified her that she nearly lost her senses. As soon as she lifted the lid, a number of hor-

rible and frightful looking demons bounced
out of the box and surrounded her as if they
intended to kill her. Not even in nightmares
had she ever seen such horrible creatures as
her much-coveted box contained. A demon
with one huge eye right in the middle of its
forehead came and glared at her, monsters
with gaping mouths looked as if they would
devour her, a huge snake coiled and hissed
about her, and a big frog hopped and croaked
towards her.

The old woman had never been so frightened in her life, and ran from the spot as fast
as her quaking legs would carry her, glad to
escape alive. When she reached home she fell
to the floor and told her husband with tears
all that had happened to her, and how she had
been nearly killed by the demons in the box.

Then she began to blame the sparrow, but
the old man stopped her at once, saying:

"Don't blame the sparrow, it is your wickedness which has at last met with its reward. I
only hope this may be a lesson to you in the
future!"

The old woman said nothing more, and
from that day she repented of her cross,
unkind ways, and by degrees became a good
old woman, so that her husband hardly knew
her to be the same person, and they spent

The old woman had never been so frightened in her life.

their last days together happily, free from want or care, spending carefully the treasure the old man had received from his pet, the tongue-cut sparrow.

The Story of
Princess Hase

A STORY OF OLD JAPAN

MANY, MANY YEARS AGO there lived in
Nara, the ancient Capital of Japan, a
wise State minister, by name Prince Toyonari
Fujiwara. His wife was a noble, good, and
beautiful woman called Princess Murasaki
(Violet). They had been married by their
respective families according to Japanese
custom when very young, and had lived
together happily ever since. They had, however, one cause for great sorrow, for as the
years went by no child was born to them. This
made them very unhappy, for they both
longed to see a child of their own who would
grow up to gladden their old age, carry on the
family name, and keep up the ancestral rites
when they were dead. The Prince and his
lovely wife, after long consultation and much
thought, determined to make a pilgrimage to
the temple of Hase-no-Kwannon (Goddess of

Mercy at Hase), for they believed, according to the beautiful tradition of their religion, that the Mother of Mercy, Kwannon, comes to answer the prayers of mortals in the form that they need the most. Surely after all these years of prayer she would come to them in the form of a beloved child in answer to their special pilgrimage, for that was the greatest need of their two lives. Everything else they had that this life could give them, but it was all as nothing because the cry of their hearts was unsatisfied.

So the Prince Toyonari and his wife went to the temple of Kwannon at Hase and stayed there for a long time, both daily offering incense and praying to Kwannon, the Heavenly Mother, to grant them the desire of their whole lives. And their prayer was answered.

A daughter was born at last to the Princess Murasaki, and great was the joy of her heart. On presenting the child to her husband they both decided to call her Hase-Hime, or the Princess of Hase, because she was the gift of the Kwannon at that place. They both reared her with great care and tenderness, and the child grew in strength and beauty.

When the little girl was five years old her mother fell dangerously ill and all the doctors and their medicines could not save her. A little before she breathed her last she called her daughter to her, and gently stroking her head, said:

"Hase-Hime, do you know that your mother cannot live any longer? Though I die, you must grow up a good girl. Do your best not to give trouble to your nurse or any other of your family. Perhaps your father will marry again and someone will fill my place as your mother. If so do not grieve for me, but look upon your father's second wife as your true mother, and be obedient and filial to both her and your father. Remember when you are grown up to be submissive to those who are your superiors, and to be kind to all those who are under you. Don't forget this. I die with the hope that you will grow up a model woman."

Hase-Hime listened in an attitude of respect while her mother spoke, and promised to do all that she was told. There is a proverb which says "As the soul is at three so it is at one hundred," and so Hase-Hime grew up as her mother had wished, a good and obedient little Princess, though she was now too young to understand how great was the loss of her mother.

Not long after the death of his first wife, Prince Toyonari married again, a lady of noble

Hase-Hime listened in an attitude of respect.

birth named Princess Terute. Very different in character, alas! to the good and wise Princess Murasaki, this woman had a cruel, bad heart. She did not love her step-daughter at all, and was often very unkind to the little motherless girl, saying to herself:

"This is not my child! this is not my child!"

But Hase-Hime bore every unkindness with patience, and even waited upon her step-mother kindly and obeyed her in every way and never gave any trouble, just as she had been trained by her own good mother, so that the Lady Terute had no cause for complaint against her.

The little Princess was very diligent, and her favourite studies were music and poetry. She would spend several hours practising every day, and her father had the most proficient of masters he could find to teach her the koto (Japanese harp), the art of writing letters and verse. When she was twelve years of age she could play so beautifully that she and her step-mother were summoned to the Palace to perform before the Emperor.

It was the Festival of the Cherry Flowers, and there were great festivities at the Court. The Emperor threw himself into the enjoyment of the season, and commanded that Princess Hase should perform before him on the koto, and that her mother Princess Terute should accompany her on the flute.

The Emperor sat on a raised daïs, before which was hung a curtain of finely-sliced bamboo and purple tassels, so that His Majesty might see all and not be seen, for no ordinary subject was allowed to look upon his sacred face.

Hase-Hime was a skilled musician though so young, and often astonished her masters by her wonderful memory and talent. On this momentous occasion she played well. But Princess Terute, her step-mother, who was a lazy woman and never took the trouble to practise daily, broke down in her accompaniment and had to request one of the Court ladies to take her place. This was a great disgrace, and she was furiously jealous to think that she had failed where her step-daughter succeeded; and to make matters worse the Emperor sent many beautiful gifts to the little Princess to reward her for playing so well at the Palace.

There was also now another reason why Princess Terute hated her step-daughter, for she had had the good fortune to have a son born to her, and in her inmost heart she kept saying:

"If only Hase-Hime were not here, my son would have all the love of his father."

And never having learned to control herself, she allowed this wicked thought to grow into the awful desire of taking her step-daughter's life.

So one day she secretly ordered some poison and poisoned some sweet wine. This poisoned wine she put into a bottle. Into another similar bottle she poured some good wine. It was the occasion of the Boys' Festival on the fifth of May, and Hase-Hime was playing with her little brother. All his toys of warriors and heroes were spread out and she was telling him wonderful stories about each of them.

They were both enjoying themselves and laughing merrily with their attendants when his mother entered with the two bottles of wine and some delicious cakes.

"You are both so good and happy," said the wicked Princess Terute with a smile, "that I have brought you some sweet wine as a reward—and here are some nice cakes for my good children."

And she filled two cups from the different bottles.

Hase-Hime, never dreaming of the dreadful part her step-mother was acting, took one of the cups of wine and gave to her little step-brother the other that had been poured out for him.

The wicked woman had carefully marked the poisoned bottle, but on coming into the room she had grown nervous, and pouring out the wine hurriedly had unconsciously given the poisoned cup to her own child. All this time she was anxiously watching the little Princess, but to her amazement no change whatever took place in the young girl's face. Suddenly the little boy screamed and threw himself on the floor, doubled up with pain. His mother flew to him, taking the precaution to upset the two tiny jars of wine which she had brought into the room, and lifted him up. The attendants rushed for the doctor, but nothing could save the child—he died within the hour in his mother's arms. Doctors did not know much in those ancient times, and it was thought that the wine had disagreed with the boy, causing convulsions of which he died.

Thus was the wicked woman punished in losing her own child when she had tried to do away with her step-daughter; but instead of blaming herself she began to hate Hase-Hime more than ever in the bitterness and wretchedness of her own heart, and she eagerly watched for an opportunity to do her harm, which was, however, long in coming.

When Hase-Hime was thirteen years of age, she had already become mentioned as a poetess of some merit. This was an accomplishment very much cultivated by the women of old Japan and one held in high esteem.

It was the rainy season at Nara, and floods were reported every day as doing damage in the neighbourhood. The river Tatsuta, which flowed through the Imperial Palace grounds, was swollen to the top of its banks, and the roaring of the torrents of water rushing along a narrow bed so disturbed the Emperor's rest day and night, that a serious nervous disorder was the result. An Imperial Edict was sent forth to all the Buddhist temples commanding the priests to offer up continuous prayers to Heaven to stop the noise of the flood. But this was of no avail.

Then it was whispered in Court circles that the Princess Hase, the daughter of Prince To-yonari Fujiwara, second minister at Court, was the most gifted poetess of the day, though still so young, and her masters confirmed the report. Long ago, a beautiful and gifted maiden-poetess had moved Heaven by praying in verse, had brought down rain upon a land famished with drought—so said the ancient biographers of the poetess Ono-no-Komachi. If the Princess Hase were to write a poem and offer it in prayer, might it not stop the noise of the rushing river and remove the cause of the Imperial illness? What the Court said at last reached the ears of the Emperor himself, and he sent an order to the minister Prince Toyonari to this effect.

Great indeed was Hase-Hime's fear and astonishment when her father sent for her and told her what was required of her. Heavy, indeed, was the duty that was laid on her young shoulders—that of saving the Emper-or's life by the merit of her verse.

At last the day came and her poem was fin-ished. It was written on a leaflet of paper heavily flecked with gold-dust. With her father

Her father told her what was required of her.

and attendants and some of the Court offi-
cials, she proceeded to the bank of the roaring torrent and raising up her heart to
Heaven, she read the poem she had com-
posed, aloud, lifting it heavenwards in her two
hands.

Strange indeed it seemed to all those standing round. The waters ceased their roaring,
and the river was quiet in direct answer to her
prayer. After this the Emperor soon recovered
his health.

His Majesty was highly pleased, and sent
for her to the Palace and rewarded her with
the rank of *Chinjo*—that of Lieutenant-

General—to distinguish her. From that time she was called Chinjo-Hime, or the Lieutenant-General Princess, and respected and loved by all.

There was only one person who was not pleased at Hase-Hime's success. That one was her step-mother. For ever brooding over the death of her own child whom she had killed when trying to poison her step-daughter, she had the mortification of seeing her rise to power and honour, marked by Imperial favour and the admiration of the whole Court. Her envy and jealousy burned in her heart like fire. Many were the lies she carried to her husband about Hase-Hime, but all to no purpose. He would listen to none of her tales, telling her sharply that she was quite mistaken.

At last the step-mother, seizing the opportunity of her husband's absence, ordered one of her old servants to take the innocent girl to the Hibari Mountains, the wildest part of the country, and to kill her there. She invented a dreadful story about the little Princess, saying that this was the only way to prevent disgrace falling upon the family—by killing her.

Katoda, her vassal, was bound to obey his mistress. Anyhow, he saw that it would be the wisest plan to pretend obedience in the absence of the girl's father, so he placed Hase-

Hime in a palanquin and accompanied her to the most solitary place he could find in the wild district. The poor child knew there was no good in protesting to her unkind step-mother at being sent away in this strange manner, so she went as she was told.

But the old servant knew that the young Princess was quite innocent of all the things her step-mother had invented to him as reasons for her outrageous orders, and he determined to save her life. Unless he killed her, however, he could not return to his cruel task-mistress, so he decided to stay out in the wilderness. With the help of some peasants he soon built a little cottage, and having sent secretly for his wife to come, these two good old people did all in their power to take care of the now unfortunate Princess. She all the time trusted in her father, knowing that as soon as he returned home and found her absent, he would search for her.

Prince Toyonari, after some weeks, came home, and was told by his wife that his daughter Hase-Hime had done something wrong and had run away for fear of being punished. He was nearly ill with anxiety. Everyone in the house told the same story—that Hase-Hime had suddenly disappeared, none of them knew why or whither. For fear of scandal he kept the matter quiet and searched everywhere he could think of, but all to no purpose.

One day, trying to forget his terrible worry, he called all his men together and told them to make ready for a several days' hunt in the mountains. They were soon ready and mounted, waiting at the gate for their lord. He rode hard and fast to the district of the Hibari Mountains, a great company following him. He was soon far ahead of everyone, and at last found himself in a narrow picturesque valley.

Looking round and admiring the scenery, he noticed a tiny house on one of the hills quite near, and then he distinctly heard a beautiful clear voice reading aloud. Seized with curiosity as to who could be studying so diligently in such a lonely spot, he dismounted, and leaving his horse to his groom, he walked up the hillside and approached the cottage. As he drew nearer his surprise increased, for he could see that the reader was a beautiful girl. The cottage was wide open and she was sitting facing the view. Listening attentively, he heard her reading the Buddhist scriptures with great devotion. More and more curious, he hurried on to the tiny gate and entered the little garden, and looking up beheld his lost daughter Hase-Hime. She was so intent on what she was saying that she neither heard nor saw her father till he spoke.

"Hase-Hime!" he cried, "it is you, my Hase-Hime!"

Taken by surprise, she could hardly realise that it was her own dear father who was calling her, and for a moment she was utterly bereft of the power to speak or move.

"My father, my father! It is indeed you—oh, my father!" was all she could say, and running to him she caught hold of his thick sleeve, and burying her face burst into a passion of tears.

Her father stroked her dark hair, asking her gently to tell him all that had happened, but she only wept on, and he wondered if he were not really dreaming.

Then the faithful old servant Katoda came out, and bowing himself to the ground before his master, poured out the long tale of wrong, telling him all that had happened, and how it was that he found his daughter in such a wild and desolate spot with only two old servants to take care of her.

The Prince's astonishment and indignation knew no bounds. He gave up the hunt at once and hurried home with his daughter. One of the company galloped ahead to inform the household of the glad news, and the step-mother hearing what had happened, and fearful of meeting her husband now that her

She could hardly realise that it was her own dear father.

wickedness was discovered, fled from the house and returned in disgrace to her father's roof, and nothing more was heard of her.

The old servant Katoda was rewarded with the highest promotion in his master's service, and lived happily to the end of his days, devoted to the little Princess, who never forgot that she owed her life to this faithful retainer. She was no longer troubled by an unkind step-mother, and her days passed happily and quietly with her father.

As Prince Toyonari had no son, he adopted a younger son of one of the Court nobles to be his heir, and to marry his daughter Hase-Hime, and in a few years the marriage took place. Hase-Hime lived to a good old age, and all said that she was the wisest, most devout, and most beautiful mistress that had ever reigned in Prince Toyonari's ancient house. She had the joy of presenting her son, the future lord of the family, to her father just before he retired from active life.

To this day there is preserved a piece of needlework in one of the Buddhist temples of Kyoto. It is a beautiful piece of tapestry, with the figure of Buddha embroidered in the silky threads drawn from the stem of the lotus. This is said to have been the work of the hands of the good Princess Hase.

The Story of Urashima Taro, the Fisher Lad

LONG, LONG AGO in the province of Tango there lived on the shore of Japan in the little fishing village of Mizu-no-ye a young fisherman named Urashima Taro. His father had been a fisherman before him, and his skill had more than doubly descended to his son, for Urashima was the most skilful fisher in all that country side, and could catch more bonito and *tai* in a day than his comrades could in a week.

But in the little fishing village, more than for being a clever fisher of the sea was he known for his kind heart. In his whole life he had never hurt anything, either great or small, and when a boy, his companions had always laughed at him, for he would never join with them in teasing animals, but always tried to keep them from this cruel sport.

One soft summer twilight he was going home at the end of a day's fishing when he came upon a group of children. They were all screaming and talking at the tops of their voices, and seemed to be in a state of great excitement about something, and on his going up to them to see what was the matter he saw that they were tormenting a tortoise. First one boy pulled it this way, then another boy pulled it that way, while a third child beat it with a stick, and the fourth hammered its shell with a stone.

Now Urashima felt very sorry for the poor tortoise and made up his mind to rescue it. He spoke to the boys:

"Look here, boys, you are treating that poor tortoise so badly that it will soon die!"

The boys, who were all of an age when children seem to delight in being cruel to animals, took no notice of Urashima's gentle reproof, but went on teasing it as before. One of the older boys answered:

"Who cares whether it lives or dies? We do not. Here, boys, go on, go on!"

And they began to treat the poor tortoise more cruelly than ever. Urashima waited a moment, turning over in his mind what would be the best way to deal with the boys. He would try to persuade them to give the tortoise up to him, so he smiled at them and said:

"I am sure you are all good, kind boys! Now

won't you give me the tortoise? I should like
to have it so much!"

"No, we won't give you the tortoise," said
one of the boys. "Why should we? We caught
it ourselves."

"What you say is true," said Urashima, "but
I do not ask you to give it to me for nothing. I
will give you some money for it—in other
words, the Ojisan (Uncle) will buy it of you.
Won't that do for you, my boys?" He held up
the money to them, strung on a piece of string
through a hole in the centre of each coin.
"Look, boys, you can buy anything you like
with this money. You can do much more with
this money than you can with that poor tortoise. See what good boys you are to listen to
me."

The boys were not bad boys at all, they
were only mischievous, and as Urashima
spoke they were won by his kind smile and
gentle words and began "to be of his spirit,"
as they say in Japan. Gradually they all came
up to him, the ringleader of the little band
holding out the tortoise to him.

"Very well, Ojisan, we will give you the tortoise if you will give us the money!" And
Urashima took the tortoise and gave the
money to the boys, who, calling to each other,
scampered away and were soon out of sight.

Then Urashima stroked the tortoise's back, saying as he did so:

"Oh, you poor thing! Poor thing!—there, there! you are safe now! They say that a stork lives for a thousand years, but the tortoise for ten thousand years. You have the longest life of any creature in this world, and you were in great danger of having that precious life cut short by those cruel boys. Luckily I was passing by and saved you, and so life is still yours. Now I am going to take you back to your home, the sea, at once. Do not let yourself be caught again, for there might be no one to save you next time!"

All the time that the kind fisherman was speaking he was walking quickly to the shore and out upon the rocks; then putting the tortoise into the water he watched the animal disappear, and turned homewards himself, for he was tired and the sun had set.

The next morning Urashima went out as usual in his boat. The weather was fine and the sea and sky were both blue and soft in the tender haze of the summer morning. Urashima got into his boat and dreamily pushed out to sea, throwing his line as he did so. He soon passed the other fishing boats and left them behind him till they were lost to sight in the distance, and his boat drifted further and further out upon the blue waters. Somehow, he knew not why, he felt unusually happy that morning; and he could not help wishing that, like the tortoise he set free the day before, he had thousands of years to live instead of his own short span of human life.

He was suddenly startled from his reverie by hearing his own name called:

"Urashima, Urashima!"

Clear as a bell and soft as the summer wind the name floated over the sea.

He stood up and looked in every direction, thinking that one of the other boats had overtaken him, but gaze as he might over the wide expanse of water, near or far there was no sign of a boat, so the voice could not have come from any human being.

Startled, and wondering who or what it was that had called him so clearly, he looked in all directions round about him and saw that without his knowing it a tortoise had come to the side of the boat. Urashima saw with surprise that it was the very tortoise he had rescued the day before.

"Well, Mr. Tortoise," said Urashima, "was it you who called my name just now?"

The tortoise nodded its head several times, and said:

"Yes, it was I. Yesterday in your honourable

shadow (*o kage sama de*) my life was saved, and I have come to offer you my thanks and to tell you how grateful I am for your kindness to me."

"Indeed," said Urashima, "that is very polite of you. Come up into the boat. I would offer you a smoke, but as you are a tortoise doubtless you do not smoke," and the fisherman laughed at the joke.

"He—he—he—he!" laughed the tortoise; "*sake* (rice wine) is my favourite refreshment, but I do not care for tobacco."

"Indeed," said Urashima, "I regret very much that I have no *sake* in my boat to offer you, but come up and dry your back in the sun—tortoises always love to do that."

So the tortoise climbed into the boat, the fisherman helping him, and after an exchange of complimentary speeches the tortoise said:

"Have you ever seen Rin Gin, the Palace of the Dragon King of the Sea, Urashima?"

The fisherman shook his head and replied: "No; year after year the sea has been my home, but though I have often heard of the Dragon King's realm under the sea I have never yet set eyes on that wonderful place. It must be very far away, if it exists at all!"

"Is that really so? You have never seen the Sea King's Palace? Then you have missed seeing one of the most wonderful sights in the whole universe. It is far away at the bottom of the sea, but if I take you there we shall soon reach the place. If you would like to see the Sea King's land I will be your guide."

"I should like to go there, certainly, and you are very kind to think of taking me, but you must remember that I am only a poor mortal and have not the power of swimming like a sea creature such as you are——"

Before the fisherman could say more the tortoise stopped him, saying:

"What? You need not swim yourself. If you will ride on my back I will take you without any trouble on your part."

"But," said Urashima, "how is it possible for me to ride on your small back?"

"It may seem absurd to you, but I assure you that you can do so. Try at once! Just come and get on my back, and see if it is as impossible as you think!"

As the tortoise finished speaking, Urashima looked at its shell, and strange to say he saw that the creature had suddenly grown so big that a man could easily sit on its back.

"This is strange indeed!" said Urashima; "then, Mr. Tortoise, with your kind permission I will get on your back. *Dokoisho!*"[1] he exclaimed as he jumped on.

---

[1] "All right" (only used by lower classes).

The tortoise, with an unmoved face, as if this strange proceeding were quite an ordinary event, said:

"Now we will set out at our leisure," and with these words he leapt into the sea with Urashima on his back. Down through the water the tortoise dived. For a long time these two strange companions rode through the sea. Urashima never grew tired, nor his clothes moist with the water. At last, far away in the distance a magnificent gate appeared, and behind the gate, the long, sloping roofs of a palace on the horizon.

"Ya," exclaimed Urashima, "that looks like the gate of some large palace just appearing! Mr. Tortoise, can you tell what that place is we can now see?"

"That is the great gate of the Rin Gin Palace. The large roof that you see behind the gate is the Sea King's Palace itself."

"Then we have at last come to the realm of the Sea King and to his Palace," said Urashima.

"Yes, indeed," answered the tortoise, "and don't you think we have come very quickly?" And while he was speaking the tortoise reached the side of the gate. "And here we are, and you must please walk from here."

The tortoise now went in front, and speak-

"That looks like the gate of some large palace!"

ing to the gatekeeper said:

"This is Urashima Taro, from the country of Japan. I have had the honour of bringing him as a visitor to this kingdom. Please show him the way."

Then the gatekeeper, who was a fish, at once led the way through the gate before them.

The red bream, the flounder, the sole, the cuttlefish, and all the chief vassals of the Dragon King of the Sea now came out with courtly bows to welcome the stranger.

"Urashima Sama, Urashima Sama! welcome to the Sea Palace, the home of the Dragon King of the Sea. Thrice welcome are you, having come from such a distant country. And you, Mr. Tortoise, we are greatly indebted to you for all your trouble in bringing Urashima here." Then, turning again to Urashima, they said, "Please follow us this way," and from here the whole band of fishes became his guides.

Urashima, being only a poor fisher lad, did not know how to behave in a palace; but, strange though it all was to him, he did not feel ashamed or embarrassed, but followed his kind guides quite calmly where they led to the inner palace. When he reached the portals a beautiful Princess with her attendant maidens came out to welcome him. She was more beautiful than any human being, and was robed in flowing garments of red and soft green like the under side of a wave, and golden threads glimmered through the folds of her gown. Her lovely black hair streamed over her shoulders in the fashion of a king's daughter many hundreds of years ago, and when she spoke her voice sounded like music over the water. Urashima was lost in wonder while he looked upon her, and he could not speak. Then he remembered that he ought to bow, but before he could make a low obeisance the Princess took him by the hand and led him to a beautiful hall, and to the seat of honour at the upper end, and bade him be seated.

"Urashima Taro, it gives me the highest pleasure to welcome you to my father's kingdom," said the Princess. "Yesterday you set free a tortoise, and I have sent for you to thank you for saving my life, for I was that tortoise. Now if you like you shall live here for ever in the land of eternal youth, where summer never dies and where sorrow never comes, and I will be your bride if you will, and we will live together happily for ever afterwards!"

And as Urashima listened to her sweet words and gazed upon her lovely face his heart was filled with a great wonder and joy, and he answered her, wondering if it was not all a dream:

"Thank you a thousand times for your kind speech. There is nothing I could wish for more than to be permitted to stay here with you in this beautiful land, of which I have often heard, but have never seen to this day. Beyond all words, this is the most wonderful place I have ever seen."

While he was speaking a train of fishes appeared, all dressed in ceremonial, trailing garments. One by one, silently and with stately steps, they entered the hall, bearing on coral trays delicacies of fish and seaweed, such as no one can dream of, and this wondrous feast was set before the bride and bridegroom. The bridal was celebrated with dazzling splendour, and in the Sea King's realm there was great rejoicing. As soon as the young pair had pledged themselves in the wedding cup of wine, three times three, music was played, and songs were sung, and fishes with silver scales and golden tails stepped in from the waves and danced. Urashima enjoyed himself with all his heart. Never in his whole life had he sat down to such a marvellous feast.

When the feast was over the Princess asked the bridegroom if he would like to walk through the palace and see all there was to be seen. Then the happy fisherman, following his bride, the Sea King's daughter, was shown all the wonders of that enchanted land where youth and joy go hand in hand and neither time nor age can touch them. The palace was built of coral and adorned with pearls, and the beauties and wonders of the place were so great that the tongue fails to describe them.

But, to Urashima, more wonderful than the palace was the garden that surrounded it. Here was to be seen at one time the scenery of the four different seasons; the beauties of summer and winter, spring and autumn, were displayed to the wondering visitor at once.

First, when he looked to the east, the plum and cherry trees were seen in full bloom, the nightingales sang in the pink avenues, and butterflies flitted from flower to flower.

Looking to the south all the trees were green in the fulness of summer, and the day cicala and the night cricket chirruped loudly.

Looking to the west the autumn maples were ablaze like a sunset sky, and the chrysanthemums were in perfection.

Looking to the north the change made Urashima start, for the ground was silver white with snow, and trees and bamboos were also covered with snow and the pond was thick with ice.

And each day there were new joys and new wonders for Urashima, and so great was his happiness that he forgot everything, even the home he had left behind and his parents and his own country, and three days passed without his even thinking of all he had left behind. Then his mind came back to him and he remembered who he was, and that he did not belong to this wonderful land or the Sea King's palace, and he said to himself:

"O dear! I must not stay on here, for I have

an old father and mother at home. What can have happened to them all this time? How anxious they must have been these days when I did not return as usual. I must go back at once without letting one more day pass." And he began to prepare for the journey in great haste.

Then he went to his beautiful wife, the Princess, and bowing low before her he said:

"Indeed, I have been very happy with you for a long time, Otohime Sama" (for that was her name), "and you have been kinder to me than any words can tell. But now I must say good-bye. I must go back to my old parents."

Then Otohime Sama began to weep, and said softly and sadly:

"Is it not well with you here, Urashima, that you wish to leave me so soon? Where is the haste? Stay with me yet another day only!"

But Urashima had remembered his old parents, and in Japan the duty to parents is stronger than everything else, stronger even than pleasure or love, and he would not be persuaded, but answered:

"Indeed, I must go. Do not think that I wish to leave you. It is not that. I must go and see my old parents. Let me go for one day and I will come back to you."

"Then," said the Princess sorrowfully,

"there is nothing to be done. I will send you back to-day to your father and mother, and instead of trying to keep you with me one more day, I shall give you this as a token of our love—please take it back with you"; and she brought him a beautiful lacquer box tied about with a silken cord and tassels of red silk.

Urashima had received so much from the Princess already that he felt some compunction in taking the gift, and said:

"It does not seem right for me to take yet another gift from you after all the many favours I have received at your hands, but because it is your wish I will do so," and then he added:

"Tell me what is this box?"

"That," answered the Princess, "is the *Tamate-Bako* (Box of the Jewel Hand), and it contains something very precious. You must not open this box, whatever happens! If you open it something dreadful will happen to you! Now promise me that you will never open this box!"

And Urashima promised that he would never, *never* open the box whatever happened.

Then bidding good-bye to Otohime Sama he went down to the seashore, the Princess and

her attendants following him, and there he
found a large tortoise waiting for him.

He quickly mounted the creature's back and
was carried away over the shining sea into the
East. He looked back to wave his hand to Otohime Sama till at last he could see her no
more, and the land of the Sea King and the
roofs of the wonderful palace were lost in the
far, far distance. Then, with his face turned
eagerly towards his own land, he looked for
the rising of the blue hills on the horizon
before him.

At last the tortoise carried him into the bay
he knew so well, and to the shore from
whence he had set out. He stepped on to the
shore and looked about him while the tortoise
rode away back to the Sea King's realm.

But what is the strange fear that seizes
Urashima as he stands and looks about him?
Why does he gaze so fixedly at the people that
pass him by, and why do they in turn stand
and look at him? The shore is the same and
the hills are the same, but the people that he
sees walking past him have very different
faces to those he had known so well before.

Wondering what it can mean he walks
quickly towards his old home. Even that looks
different, but a house stands on the spot, and
he calls out:

"Father, I have just returned!" and he was about to enter, when he saw a strange man coming out.

"Perhaps my parents have moved while I have been away, and have gone somewhere else," was the fisherman's thought. Somehow he began to feel strangely anxious, he could not tell why.

"Excuse me," said he to the man who was staring at him, "but till within the last few days I have lived in this house. My name is Urashima Taro. Where have my parents gone whom I left here?"

A very bewildered expression came over the face of the man, and, still gazing intently on Urashima's face, he said:

"What? Are you Urashima Taro?"

"Yes," said the fisherman, "I am Urashima Taro!"

"Ha, ha!" laughed the man, "you must not make such jokes. It is true that once upon a time a man called Urashima Taro did live in this village, but that is a story three hundred years old. He could not possibly be alive now!"

When Urashima heard these strange words he was frightened, and said:

"Please, please, you must not joke with me, for I am greatly perplexed. I am really Urashima Taro, and I certainly have not lived three hundred years. Till four or five days ago I lived on this spot. Tell me what I want to know without more joking, please."

But the man's face grew more and more grave, and he answered:

"You may or may not be Urashima Taro, I don't know. But the Urashima Taro of whom I have heard is a man who lived three hundred years ago. Perhaps you are his spirit come to re-visit your old home?"

"Why do you mock me?" said Urashima. "I am no spirit! I am a living man—do you not see my feet"; and "don-don," he stamped on the ground, first with one foot and then with the other to show the man. (Japanese ghosts have no feet.)

"But Urashima Taro lived three hundred years ago, that is all I know; it is written in the village chronicles," persisted the man, who could not believe what the fisherman said.

Urashima was lost in bewilderment and trouble. He stood looking all around him, terribly puzzled, and, indeed, something in the appearance of everything was different to what he remembered before he went away, and the awful feeling came over him that what the man said was perhaps true. He seemed to be in a strange dream. The few days he had spent in the Sea King's palace beyond the sea had not been days at all; they had been hundreds of years, and in that time his parents had died and all the people he had ever known, and the village had written down his story. There was no use in staying here any longer. He must get back to his beautiful wife beyond the sea.

He made his way back to the beach, carrying in his hand the box which the Princess had given him. But which was the way? He could not find it alone! Suddenly he remembered the box, the *Tamate-Bako*.

"The Princess told me when she gave me the box never to open it—that it contained a very precious thing. But now that I have no home, now that I have lost everything that was dear to me here, and my heart grows thin with sadness, at such a time, if I open the box, surely I shall find something that will help me, something that will show me the way back to my beautiful Princess over the sea. There is nothing else for me to do now. Yes, yes, I will open the box and look in!"

And so his heart consented to this act of disobedience, and he tried to persuade himself that he was doing the right thing in breaking his promise.

Slowly, very slowly, he untied the red silk

Only a beautiful little purple cloud rose out of the box.

cord, slowly and wonderingly he lifted the lid of the precious box. And what did he find? Strange to say only a beautiful little purple cloud rose out of the box in three soft wisps. For an instant it covered his face and wavered over him as if loth to go, and then it floated away like vapour over the sea.

Urashima, who had been till that moment like a strong and handsome youth of twenty-four, suddenly became very, very old. His back doubled up with age, his hair turned snowy white, his face wrinkled and he fell down dead on the beach.

Poor Urashima! because of his disobedience he could never return to the Sea King's realm or the lovely Princess beyond the sea.

Little children, never be disobedient to those who are wiser than you, for disobedience was the beginning of all the miseries and sorrows of life.

The Ogre of Rashomon

LONG, LONG AGO in Kyoto, the people of the city were terrified by accounts of a dreadful ogre, who, it was said, haunted the Gate of Rashomon at twilight and seized whoever passed by. The missing victims were never seen again, so it was whispered that the ogre was a horrible cannibal, who not only killed the unhappy victims but ate them also. Now everybody in the town and neighbourhood was in great fear, and no one durst venture out after sunset near the Gate of Rashomon.

Now at this time there lived in Kyoto a general named Raiko, who had made himself famous for his brave deeds. Some time before this he made the country ring with his name, for he had attacked Oeyama, where a band of ogres lived with their chief, who instead of wine drank the blood of human beings. He had routed them all and cut off the head of the chief monster.

This brave warrior was always followed by a band of faithful knights. In this band there were five knights of great valour. One evening as the five knights sat at a feast quaffing *sake* in their rice bowls and eating all kinds of fish, raw, and stewed, and broiled, and toasting each other's healths and exploits, the first knight, Hojo, said to the others:

"Have you all heard the rumour that every evening after sunset there comes an ogre to the Gate of Rashomon, and that he seizes all who pass by?"

The second knight, Watanabe, answered him, saying:

"Do not talk such nonsense! All the ogres were killed by our chief Raiko at Oeyama! It cannot be true, because even if any ogres did escape from that great killing they would not dare to show themselves in this city, for they know that our brave master would at once attack them if he knew that any of them were still alive!"

"Then do you disbelieve what I say, and think that I am telling you a falsehood?"

"No, I do not think that you are telling a lie," said Watanabe; "but you have heard some old woman's story which is not worth believing."

"Then the best plan is to prove what I say, by going there yourself and finding out yourself whether it is true or not," said Hojo.

Watanabe, the second knight, could not bear the thought that his companion should believe he was afraid, so he answered quickly:

"Of course, I will go at once and find out for myself!"

So Watanabe at once got ready to go—he buckled on his long sword and put on a coat of armour, and tied on his large helmet. When he was ready to start he said to the others:

"Give me something so that I can prove I have been there!"

Then one of the men got a roll of writing paper and his box of Indian ink and brushes, and the four comrades wrote their names on a piece of paper.

"I will take this," said Watanabe, "and put it on the Gate of Rashomon, so to-morrow morning will you all go and look at it? I may be able to catch an ogre or two by then!" and he mounted his horse and rode off gallantly.

It was a very dark night, and there was neither moon nor star to light Watanabe on his way. To make the darkness worse a storm came on, the rain fell heavily and the wind howled like wolves in the mountains. Any ordinary man would have trembled at the thought of going out of doors, but Watanabe was a brave warrior and dauntless, and his honour and word were at stake, so he sped on into the night, while his companions listened to the sound of his horse's hoofs dying away in the distance, then shut the sliding shutters close and gathered round the charcoal fire and wondered what would happen—and whether their comrade would encounter one of those horrible *oni*.

At last Watanabe reached the Gate of Rashomon, but peer as he might through the darkness he could see no sign of an ogre.

"It is just as I thought," said Watanabe to himself; "there are certainly no ogres here; it is only an old woman's story. I will stick this paper on the gate so that the others can see I have been here when they come to-morrow, and then I will take my way home and laugh at them all."

He fastened the piece of paper, signed by all his four companions, on the gate, and then turned his horse's head towards home.

As he did so he became aware that someone was behind him, and at the same time a voice called out to him to wait. Then his helmet was seized from the back.

"Who are you?" said Watanabe fearlessly. He then put out his hand and groped around to find out who or what it was that held him by the helmet. As he did so he touched something that felt like an arm—it was covered with hair and as big round as the trunk of a tree!

Watanabe knew at once that this was the arm of an ogre, so he drew his sword and cut at it fiercely.

There was a loud yell of pain, and then the ogre dashed in front of the warrior.

Watanabe's eyes grew large with wonder, for he saw that the ogre was taller than the great gate, his eyes were flashing like mirrors in the sunlight, and his huge mouth was wide open, and as the monster breathed, flames of fire shot out of his mouth.

The ogre thought to terrify his foe, but Watanabe never flinched. He attacked the ogre with all his strength, and thus they fought face to face for a long time. At last the ogre, finding that he could neither frighten nor beat Watanabe and that he might himself be beaten, took to flight. But Watanabe, determined not to let the monster escape, put spurs to his horse and gave chase.

But though the knight rode very fast the ogre ran faster, and to his disappointment he found himself unable to overtake the monster, who was gradually lost to sight.

Watanabe returned to the gate where the fierce fight had taken place, and got down from his horse. As he did so he stumbled upon something lying on the ground.

Stooping to pick it up he found that it was one of the ogre's huge arms which he must

Watanabe returned to the gate.

have slashed off in the fight. His joy was great at having secured such a prize, for this was the best of all proofs of his adventure with the ogre. So he took it up carefully and carried it home as a trophy of his victory.

When he got back, he showed the arm to his comrades who one and all called him the hero of their band and gave him a great feast. His wonderful deed was soon noised abroad in Kyoto, and people from far and near came to see the ogre's arm.

Watanabe now began to grow uneasy as to how he should keep the arm in safety, for he knew that the ogre to whom it belonged was still alive. He felt sure that one day or other, as soon as the ogre got over his scare, he would come to try to get his arm back again. Watanabe therefore had a box made of the strongest wood and banded with iron. In this he placed the arm, and then he sealed down the heavy lid, refusing to open it for anyone. He kept the box in his own room and took charge of it himself, never allowing it out of his sight.

Now one night he heard someone knocking at the porch, asking for admittance.

When the servant went to the door to see who it was, there was only an old woman, very respectable in appearance. On being

*Someone knocking at the porch, asking for
admittance.*

asked who she was and what was her busi-
ness, the old woman replied with a smile that
she had been nurse to the master of the house
when he was a little baby. If the lord of the
house were at home she begged to be allowed
to see him.

The servant left the old woman at the door
and went to tell his master that his old nurse
had come to see him. Watanabe thought it
strange that she should come at that time of
night, but at the thought of his old nurse, who
had been like a foster-mother to him and
whom he had not seen for a long time, a very
tender feeling sprang up for her in his heart.
He ordered the servant to show her in.

The old woman was ushered into the room, and after the customary bows and greetings were over, she said:

"Master, the report of your brave fight with the ogre at the Gate of Rashomon is so widely known that even your poor old nurse has heard of it. Is it really true, what everyone says, that you cut off one of the ogre's arms? If you did, your deed is highly to be praised!"

"I was very disappointed," said Watanabe, "that I was not able to take the monster captive, which was what I wished to do, instead of only cutting off an arm!"

"I am very proud to think," answered the old woman, "that my master was so brave as to dare to cut off an ogre's arm. There is nothing that can be compared to your courage. Before I die it is the great wish of my life to see this arm," she added pleadingly.

"No," said Watanabe, "I am sorry, but I cannot grant your request."

"But why?" asked the old woman.

"Because," replied Watanabe, "ogres are very revengeful creatures, and if I open the box there is no telling but that the ogre may suddenly appear and carry off his arm. I have had a box made on purpose with a very strong lid, and in this box I keep the ogre's arm secure; and I never show it to anyone, whatever happens."

"Your precaution is very reasonable," said the old woman. "But I am your old nurse, so surely you will not refuse to show *me* the arm. I have only just heard of your brave act, and not being able to wait till the morning I came at once to ask you to show it to me."

Watanabe was very troubled at the old woman's pleading, but he still persisted in refusing. Then the old woman said:

"Do you suspect me of being a spy sent by the ogre?"

"No, of course I do not suspect you of being the ogre's spy, for you are my old nurse," answered Watanabe.

"Then you cannot surely refuse to show me the arm any longer," entreated the old woman; "for it is the great wish of my heart to see for once in my life the arm of an ogre!"

Watanabe could not hold out in his refusal any longer, so he gave in at last, saying:

"Then I will show you the ogre's arm, since you so earnestly wish to see it. Come, follow me!" and he led the way to his own room, the old woman following.

When they were both in the room Watanabe shut the door carefully, and then going towards a big box which stood in a corner of the room, he took off the heavy lid. He then called to the old woman to come near and look in, for he never took the arm out of the box.

"What is it like? Let me have a good look at it," said the old nurse, with a joyful face.

She came nearer and nearer, as if she were afraid, till she stood right against the box. Suddenly she plunged her hand into the box and seized the arm, crying with a fearful voice which made the room shake:

"Oh, joy! I have got my arm back again!"

And from an old woman she was suddenly transformed into the towering figure of the frightful ogre!

Watanabe sprang back and was unable to move for a moment, so great was his astonishment; but recognising the ogre who had attacked him at the Gate of Rashomon, he determined with his usual courage to put an end to him this time. He seized his sword, drew it out of its sheath in a flash, and tried to cut the ogre down.

So quick was Watanabe that the creature had a narrow escape. But the ogre sprang up to the ceiling, and bursting through the roof, disappeared in the mist and clouds.

In this way the ogre escaped with his arm. The knight gnashed his teeth with disappointment, but that was all he could do. He waited in patience for another opportunity to des-

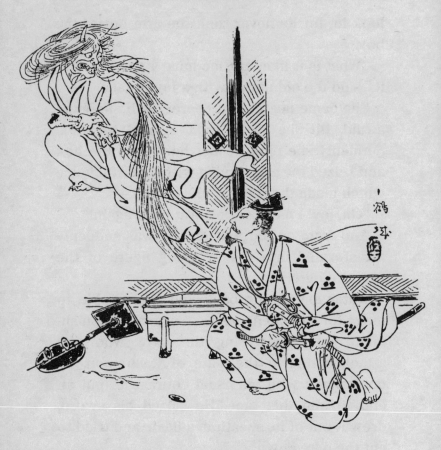

In this way the ogre escaped with his arm.

patch the ogre. But the latter was afraid of Watanabe's great strength and daring, and never troubled Kyoto again. So once more the people of the city were able to go out without fear even at night time, and the brave deeds of Watanabe have never been forgotten!